STOP BULLYING:

10 Strategies for Women to Reduce Stress Caused by Bullying at Work

Natalie Disque

ISBN: 1523299754
ISBN-13: 978-1523299751

DEDICATION

I would like to dedicate this to all people, women and men, who have had to deal with bullying in the workplace. May this book help you cope with the bully and stand your ground. Do not let them waste any more of your time by trying to put you down. You are worth more than that!

TABLE OF CONTENTS

ACKNOWLEDGMENTS

I would like to acknowledge that I have personally dealt with
bullies, both in the workplace, in school and in life. They suck!
Sorry, but there is no other way to put it.
I don't claim to know everything there is about dealing with
bullying. However, after much research, I put together this book to
help others deal with bullying better. I hope you get some worth
from the research I put into this book.

CHAPTER 1: INTRODUCTION

Getting bullied is usually something we associate with school, but it can actually happen at any time in life. Most definitions of bullying describe it as a harmful behavior, directed toward a target by a perpetrator. That behavior is usually repeated and happens often. The target is usually just one isolated person, but it can also be a group. The perpetrator can also be either one person or a group. Sometimes, they even coerce others into joining in on the bullying, even if they would otherwise not do anything to harm the target.

Bullying can cause harm in a lot of ways. In every case, it causes psychological and emotional harm. But it can also cause physical harm and interfere with a person's life in serious ways. This is why there has been so much effort recently to end bullying in schools. However, less attention has been paid to bullying in the workplace, which can be just as harmful and cause real long term damage.

Bullying in the workplace usually involves threats, humiliation, intimidation, and other types of verbal abuse. It also often involves sabotage and work interference so that the target can't do their job as well as he or she normally would.

Workplace bullying is a serious problem. If it's happening to you, it's important to take the right steps to deal with it. If you notice it happening to someone else, you should reach out and help that person. By fighting back against bullying, wherever you see it happening, you can help to make your work environment happier, healthier, and more productive.

Of course, this is not an easy issue. It might be your boss or another superior who is doing the bullying. If not, you might be in a work environment where that sort of behavior goes unpunished or is even encouraged. The bully might have important superiors on his or her side, which makes it seemingly impossible to make sure the bully is punished appropriately.

Unfortunately, more than half of the employees who report being bullied are women. Even more shocking is that about 40% of all bullies in the workplace are women themselves. The pressure women experience in a business environment that is still suffering from outdated, sexist practices is still a real problem. It has turned many women into victims of bullying and still others into bullies in their own right. You'll learn more about these deeper issues behind bullying in the next chapter.

The important thing to know is that you are not alone. And if you see someone else getting bullied, make sure they know they are not alone. There are ways to deal with this that are smart, healthy, and effective. It's not easy. These situations never are. But it is definitely worth the effort to make sure you handle this right.

This book was written to help you achieve just that. In the following chapters, you are going to learn a lot of important and effective strategies for dealing with workplace bullying. You will get a total of 10 strategies, which focus on helping you achieve a combination of stronger mental health and toughness with practical tools for making sure that the bully is properly punished for their harmful behavior.

Before that, however, you will learn more about the problem of bullying itself. It's important to have a better understanding of the problem in order to effectively deal with it. So, continue reading and as you do so, keep your own situation in mind. By relating your own situation to what you learn in this book, you'll be able to develop the right tools to deal with your problem.

CHAPTER 2: UNDERSTANDING BULLYING IN THE WORKPLACE

In the introduction, bullying was broadly defined as any behavior that causes harm to the person it is targeted toward. In the workplace, this is usually in the form of verbal abuse, threats, intimidation, and humiliation. It might also involve sabotage and other action that prevents the target from getting their work done as well as they could.

The specific behaviors that are involved in bullying can vary, depending on the specific situation. However, there are some shared characteristics that are usually involved in most cases of workplace bullying. Let's take a closer look at what is happening behind the scenes in a case of workplace bullying.

Characteristics of Bullying

There are 5 key characteristics of bullying. They may not all be present in every single case to the same degree but they are there.

The 5 characteristics are:

- The behavior is driven by a need to be in control.

- It is premeditated or planned.

- It involves an act of omission or commission (this will be explained in more detail shortly).

- It escalates as others side with the bully (whether voluntarily or by force).

- The behavior undermines business because the bully puts their personal agenda above business needs and goals.

A bully is someone who needs to feel in control. They take that control by force, likely because they couldn't get it any other way. Underneath this need for control is a feeling that they don't actually have control. In other words, they are probably secretly feeling powerless, or at least afraid of becoming powerless, so they take that anxiety out through bullying behavior that makes them feel in control.

In reality, bullying is a false sense of control because the bully ends up inspiring anger and resentment. The first opportunity employees have to get rid of the bully, they will do so. In this way, it is only a short term sense of control. This insecurity can cause a perpetual need to bully. They will use threats and intimidation to coerce their targets into doing what they want.

This bullying behavior is usually premeditated or planned. That means that they are actively seeking out opportunities to bully. They tend to approach every encounter with a bullying attitude, looking for ways to sabotage or interfere in their target's life. This means that they do not need to be provoked by the target in any way. They will bully the person, whether or not that person resists or fights back. In fact, they will even continue bullying the person when that person is compliant and agrees to the bully's demands.

Since the behavior has already been planned and decided upon in advance, there is really no response the target can make that would effectively prevent it. This is not to say that the target should give up and lose all hope. It just means that you will probably not stop a bully by trying to reason with the bully directly. Instead, you need to focus on other strategies, which you'll learn about in the next 10 chapters.

In addition to verbal forms of bullying, like verbal abuse, intimidation, humiliation, and threatening, bullies often also act through commission or omission. To act through commission is another way of saying that the bully actively does something to interfere with your work or harm you. This might mean spreading rumors, continuously distracting you from work, or even physically stopping you from doing your work. However, it's always done as a means of personally sabotaging the target, even if that happens at the expense of the business.

Acts of omission achieve the same outcome—to sabotage the target by interfering with work. However, instead of actively interfering, the bully interferes passively by refusing to act. This might mean withholding the resources you need to get your work done, or refusing to sign off on something so that you can get started. Whether through commission or omission, the bully tries to prevent work from getting done. This harms not only the target, but also the company as a whole.

Bullying doesn't usually just stop on its own. If it goes unpunished, it will only escalate and get worse. Usually, as the bully continues to behave this way without consequence, they get more and more bold and will start to enlist others into their cause of torment. In some cases, others will voluntarily join in on the bullying. However, in many cases, the bully actually coerces and forces others to support and engage in bullying behavior, even though they don't really want to. This can turn one isolated case of bullying into an office wide problem that ends up transforming the entire work environment into a negative and hostile place. This is one of the many reasons that it is important to identify and punish all acts of bullying.

Another of the many reasons a company should actively fight against bullying among its employees is that bullying is simply bad for business. Bullying undermines business because the bully puts their personal agenda above business objectives. When a bully tries to prevent their target from working as well as they could, they do it because they personally want to see that person fail, even if it means putting the entire business at risk.

As bullying escalates, the harm it can do to the company worsens. Once the office is taken over by an environment of bullying rather than of collaboration, it will severely interfere with the employees' ability to get work done or to do it to the best of their ability. Employees need an encouraging and positive environment, not a stressful and cutthroat one, in order to flourish and fulfill their potential.

Signs of Bullying

Sometimes, when you are the victim of bullying, you might think—or someone might be trying to convince you—that this is just normal work stress. However, there are some telltale signs that distinguish regular work stress from actual harmful bullying. Understand and check for these signs in yourself and your coworkers. First, let's look at signs that you will notice while at work:

- No matter how much effort you put in and how much you accomplish, it is never good enough to satisfy your bully.
- Your coworkers have been told to stop working with you, socializing with you, or talking to you.

- The bully's actions seem to be personally directed at you and actually slow down or prevent business from going smoothly.
- You feel perpetually agitated or anxious while at work.

When bullying is happening, its effects don't just stop when you leave the office. It continues to affect you even when you get home.

Here are some signs to check for when you aren't at work:

- You feel nauseous, ill, or extremely anxious before you start the work week.
- Your friends and family tell you that you obsess about work too much.
- You have high blood pressure or other health problems.
- You feel ashamed to talk to people about how you are being treated at work.
- You feel exhausted or lethargic during your time off.

- You have lost interest in your hobbies or other activities which you used to enjoy.

Yes, sometimes work is just stressful or you have a high pressure job. But if you are feeling this stressed, anxious, or depressed because of a specific person or a specific group of people, it is not just normal stress. It is workplace bullying and you should start to take the steps necessary to deal with it.

Characteristics of Targets

The people who are most often targeted by bullying have a few characteristics in common. But, they aren't the characteristics you might think they are. Typically, when we think of bully victims, we imagine a schoolyard bullying situation. The target is whoever is the weakest. In the office, however, this changes. The target is usually someone who is especially good at their job and has a lot of potential.

Here are some of the characteristics that many targets of bullying tend to share:

- The bully feels that the target poses a threat to them.

- The target is usually one of the more skilled or talented employees in the office. These people are usually bullied by their bosses or other coworkers, who feel that their job security is threatened by the target's skill.

- The target might be a whistleblower, or potential whistleblower, on inappropriate or illegal activities in the office.

- The target is usually seen as an outsider.

- The target might be "easily exploited." In other words, they have a very pro-social personality that gives them an innate desire to help, teach, or nurture others.

In short, the targets of workplace bullying are usually those who threaten to transform the workplace into a more productive, more encouraging environment in which bullying would not be a tolerated or successful strategy.

Women and Bullying

A little over half (58%) of all targets of bullying are female. This is an unfortunate symptom of a business world that is still working to overcome its sexist past. One of the reasons that women are bullied more often than men is that women are expected to behave exactly as a target of bullying does. They are expected to be passive and submissive. They are expected to avoid leadership positions and accept the working conditions they are given, rather than assertively change them.

In short, they are already seen as targets from the outset. First of all, from birth, women are encouraged to develop a very pro-social personality that can be "easily exploited" by a bully as mentioned above. This can put the average woman at a higher risk of being bullied in the workplace.

Furthermore, women are often seen as outsiders in an environment that is traditionally dominated by men. This means that they are already singled out as someone who might shake up the system, simply because of their gender. By assuming that women are more likely to be caring, nurturing, and compassionate people, some might also assume that women are more likely to be whistleblowers. Because of this, bullies will see them as a threat to their job security.

This is not to say that all women are targets of bullying. It simply highlights the ways in which the current cultural beliefs tend to assume that women fulfill certain traits and stereotypes. These assumptions tend to single women out as prime targets for bullying.

The Problem of Woman on Woman Bullying

At 62% men are definitely more likely to be bullies than women. However, that still means that roughly 40% of bullies are women. This figure may seem surprising but, in an environment where men are still largely in control, women are under increased pressure to take control however they can.

The biggest problem of having female bullies in the office is that their targets are usually also female. While male bullies target men and women more or less equally, female bullies almost always target other women in the office. In fact, 80% of employees targeted by female bullies are female themselves.

One of the reasons for this phenomenon is that female employees are usually put in competition with each other rather than allowed to collaborate. While women are becoming more commonplace, men still make up the majority. This is especially true as you climb up the ladder. This can make women who are higher up on the ladder feel that an ambitious woman, lower down the ladder, is a potential threat to her position, rather than a potential partner.

Bullying by women might also be caused by a woman's need to show dominance, even more strongly than men. Because women are usually assumed to be submissive and nurturing, it is more challenging for them to gain respect as an authority figure in the office. They may resort to bullying behavior in order to compensate for it.

By understanding the causes of bullying better, you do not need to necessarily sympathize with the bully. This information just helps you to better understand the circumstances which you are facing so that you are better prepared to deal with them.

CHAPTER 3: STRATEGY 1 - GET EDUCATED

Since you are reading this book, you probably already understand the importance of learning as much as you can about workplace bullying. As a woman, it is especially important because you risk being discredited as "overly sensitive", or just not "strong enough", to handle the competitive world of business.

Do not let anyone make you doubt yourself. There is a clear difference between healthy competition and bullying. Competition is done with respect for those who you are competing with. Healthy competition motivates you and encourages you to do your personal best. It doesn't make you dread showing up at work. It doesn't make you feel like your work is consistently not good enough. And it doesn't feel like a personal vendetta.

With this book, you have already gained a deeper understanding of what workplace bullying is, what it looks like, and how it affects you as a target. You know the signs of bullying so you know that what you are dealing with is, in fact, bullying and not just "healthy competition", as some people are surely going to try to tell you.

The more educated you get on this issue, the more confident you will be in your own perception and understanding of the situation. The confidence of understanding and knowledge is one of the main advantages of getting educated. But it also helps in a lot of other ways.

For example, by reading through the various strategies in this book, you are getting useful information and advice to help you formulate a plan for addressing the bully in your life. You shouldn't just stop with this book, however, seek out information from a lot of different resources.

Get in touch with people who have dealt with and overcome workplace bullying in their own lives. Read other books on this issue. Consult professionals and experts on this issue. Get as much information as you can, so that you can be sure you are approaching your situation as effectively as possible.

With the internet, getting educated on this issue is easier than ever before. There is an abundance of resources at your fingertips. Take advantage of it. Do plenty of research and know this issue inside and out and from every possible angle.

You don't just want to read a lot of information and leave it at that. You also need to take notes. Get a notebook dedicated to this purpose. Note down the most important information for you and remember to note what source you got that information from in case you want to reference it again later.

After taking thorough notes, you'll want to read through your notes a few times over, and then try to create an executive summary of sorts. What are the most important ideas that come up consistently throughout your notes? What are the key lessons that you have learned? What are the best tips and strategies that you have learned about in the research process?

From that, you can begin to brainstorm an action plan for dealing with your bully. Start by jotting down some notes about your situation. Make sure to include answers for the following questions:

- Who is your bully?
- What is their job title?
- How well respected (or not) are they in the office?
- Does he or she have any collaborators?
- Which bullying strategies do they seem to rely on the most?

- What do you know about their motives?

- How long has this been going on?

You can compare the details of your particular situation to the information you have learned in your research. Then, pick and choose the strategies that make the most sense and develop a clear and concrete action plan.

Make sure you don't neglect yourself in this process. A lot of books and resources that talk about workplace bullying focus exclusively on the practical matters. These are, of course, very important. However, it is equally important to focus on your emotional and physical health, so that you have the strength and mental clarity to actually execute the plan you have created.

Reading this book is an important part of this process of getting educated, so you are already on the right track. If you haven't been taking notes up to this point, stop reading for a minute and go get a notebook and pen so that you can start taking notes.

It might sound like an exhaustive process to go through all of that, but it is the best way to guarantee that you are approaching this problem in the most proactive and efficient way possible. Dealing with a bully in the workplace can be a complicated and difficult issue, especially if you can't count on very much support from your company. So you need to be thorough and confident that you are doing everything that you possibly can and you are doing it in the best way that you possibly could.

CHAPTER 4: DON'T RESPOND EMOTIONALLY

The most important thing to keep in mind when you are dealing with a bully is to not respond emotionally. This does not mean you aren't allowed to have emotions. It just means that you need to stay cool and collected when responding to your bully. You do not want to let them see how they are affecting you. You also don't want them to learn what your particular trigger points are. Bullies feed on this type of emotion and it just makes them feel more powerful.

By staying calm, you are taking back some of the control from the bully. You are taking back control of the situation and you are giving yourself a measure of power. By responding with calm reason rather than emotion, you are making sure that nobody can misinterpret what is going on. If you allow yourself to lose control, the bully can easily twist your actions to make you look like the one who is in the wrong.

I am not saying that you have to bottle up your emotions and become a robot. You just have to remain calm and rational in the moment. Afterward, you can find a private place to let it out, or call up a friend to vent. But in that moment, you need to take a deep breath and behave as if the bully is not affecting you.

The last thing you need right now is for the bully to accuse you of being the aggressive one. Even in the best case scenario, responding emotionally could end up making others believe you are "overly sensitive" because they may not have seen the extent of bullying that brought you to that point.

Of course, this is not to say that your emotions are wrong or a sign of weakness. It just means that you need to be the one in control. Don't let your decisions and actions be ruled by your emotions.

Now, I do understand, from being in these type of bullying situations myself, that this advice is definitely easier said than done. Emotions can be very powerful, especially if they have been building up over an extended period of bullying. At some point, you've just had it and you feel like you can't hold them back anymore. This is why you need to make sure you deal with your emotions as you go, so that you can avoid getting overwhelmed by them in the moments that count.

To make this a little bit easier, you might find it useful to follow some of the tips below for staying in control of your emotions. First, let's talk about what you should do during your time away from the bully:

- Talk through your feelings: talk to a close friend or relative (perhaps even a therapist) about the frustrations, anxieties, and stress you are feeling. Don't be afraid to lose control a bit in these moments. This is when it is safe to let your emotions out. Make sure your friend or relative knows that they don't need to provide solutions for you. You just need someone to listen to you vent so you can purge the emotions that have built up. After purging, you'll feel calmer and have the strength to face another day.

- Punch something: emotional energy and physical energy come from the same source. This is why emotions can cause actual physical reactions like shivering, nausea, sweating, and so on. Try enrolling in a kickboxing class or just get a punching bag so that you can beat the living daylights out of something. I have done this with pillows – they work just as good and you don't hurt yourself. Just make sure to let it all out. This will give you a similar feeling of purging and release as talking through your feelings. In some cases, releasing physical energy can be even more effective because it gives you the cathartic feeling that you've actually done something. Not to mention it can be a great workout!

- Write it down: keep a journal of your thoughts and feelings. This is another way to release emotion, and the biggest advantage here is that you'll have a written record of your bully's behavior, in addition to the effects it has had on you. This might become important as you try to prove your case and bring your bully to justice.

As much as you work on releasing your emotions, and making sure nothing gets built up, there will be some moments with your bully that just send you from 0 to 100 in no time. Here are some tips for remaining calm and maintaining reason, even in the most high stress situations with your bully:

- Keep your mouth shut: avoid responding immediately to your bully, especially if they say something particularly awful or infuriating. Always take a moment to first consider what the best and most rational response would be. That doesn't mean stare silently for minutes on end, but a few seconds pause will not be a problem, and it can stop you from saying something overly emotional and reactionary.

- Give firm, short responses: don't be terse or rude, but give responses that directly and clearly address what the bully has said. For example, if they are criticizing you, simply state "I will take note of your concerns for the future." Answering rudely or vaguely could instigate further abuse. So be brief, direct, and avoid emotional language. Put on your best business professional attitude and stick with it until the interaction is over.

- Look your bully in the eyes: when you respond, make direct eye contact (or cheat and look at their eyebrows). This will give everything you say a subtle air of confidence, which can shorten the interaction. Bullies prey on signs of weakness, so showing confidence and pure reason in these interactions will give them less fuel to keep going.

CHAPTER 5: STRATEGY 3 – CONTINUE TO DO YOUR BEST WORK

Your bully is going to be trying as hard as he or she can to make you compromise your work so that you look bad. They will withhold the resources you need. They will put up roadblocks every step of the way. They will discourage you, humiliate you, and intimidate you. They will distract you. Be aware that one of their main end goals is to make you less efficient and less productive at work. Ultimately, they probably want you to quit.

This means it is very important to make sure that they do not get that satisfaction. Keep putting your best effort into your work. In fact, try to channel that negative energy from bullying in a way that supercharges you and makes you work even harder. The more your work improves, the more control and leverage you have in the company.

For example, suppose it is your supervisor who is bullying you. If you allow this to affect your work and start being less productive, your boss can easily go to his or her supervisors and accuse you of being a bad employee. On the other hand, if your work stays consistently strong (or even improves), he or she will have nothing to make you look bad. Instead, you'll be in a stronger position to fight back.

Keeping up your work productivity is far from the easiest thing you need to do. Your bully is going to be actively fighting against you on exactly this front. That means that even maintaining an average level of productivity will be harder for you because you have someone pushing against you and trying to hold you down. It's like running a marathon while carrying a bowling ball.

This means that in order to stay a strong employee, you have to actually become stronger yourself. Staying healthy (strategy 5) is going to be a big part of that. This is because, as mentioned, physical and emotional strength are strongly tied together. So the healthier you are physically, the more strength you'll have to endure the extra stress you are enduring.

In addition, you can try following some of these tips at work:

- Go above their head: if your bully is trying to put up obstacles or withhold resources, get what you need from someone else. Remember not to do it in a way that puts blame on the bully directly. Don't say "so and so won't sign off on this." Instead, just come directly to that person for what you need and leave the bully out of it altogether.
- Work near others: when possible, do your work in communal spaces, or at least in plain view of your coworkers. This has two effects. First, it gives you a

team of eyewitnesses who can confirm that you are a dedicated worker. Secondly, it ensures that whenever your bully speaks to you, you will have witnesses to verify the abusive treatment. So try to avoid isolating yourself behind a closed office door. Take your work to the break room or leave your office door open.

- Take your work home: if it's impossible to work at the office, take some work home with you. This is, of course, not an ideal situation since you do need some time off so don't do this on a daily basis. But, this will help you stay productive in the short term until you manage to get a more permanent solution to your problem.

- Record the abuse (only in a public place): Most of us have smart phones, which also have a voice recording feature. It is usually located in the Extras area and may be called "Voice Memos". Keep your phone handy and whenever the bully approaches, click record. Save the memo recordings with dates. This way, if there wasn't a witness around to hear the abuse, you have it all recorded and can play it back when needed. An advantage of recording memos on your phone is that you can email or text it to someone, since the file is a normal mp3 or mp4 file. This makes for easy distribution of proof when needed. It also allows you to send it to your own email to keep an extra copy, should something happen to your phone recordings.

The two strategies that you have read about so far, and the remaining eight that you will read about in this book, are not meant as standalone strategies. They should be done in combination with each other. Maintaining a high level of productivity while you are dealing with a bully will not work for the long term. You will burn yourself out if you do this for an extended period.

However, maintaining strong work performance, at the same time that you use the other strategies in this book to put an end to the bullying, will help your effort. It will ensure that you remain a strong and valuable addition to the team in the eyes of your supervisors. This will help, as they will be more likely to cooperate with you when it comes to addressing the bullying you have been dealing with.

CHAPTER 6: FIND HEALTHY COPING MECHANISMS

Staying on top of your game at work and remaining in control of your emotions will be much more manageable if you establish a set of healthy coping mechanisms. This is something you need to do consciously and, unfortunately, there's no one right answer. What works for one person will be totally useless for another. Some people really do well with mediations, for example, while others find it dull and impossible.

If you don't consciously work to find healthy coping mechanisms, you will end up adopting unhealthy and harmful ones. It is your natural inclination to cope with the stress in your life somehow. If you don't make sure you are doing that in a healthy way, you could end up finding yourself binge eating junk food, drinking excessively, or engaging in other negative and harmful coping mechanisms.

If you already have negative coping mechanisms, you need to make an effort to replace them with positive ones. If you already have positive coping mechanisms, keep them up and, if they don't feel like enough, look for some more.

A coping mechanism is anything you do to release stress, relax, and feel better. That could mean going for a run or sitting down to watch your favorite TV show. Just make sure that it makes you feel good and does not cause harm to you physically, emotionally, or financially.

If you aren't sure what a good healthy coping mechanism for you is, you'll have to go through a bit of an experimental phase. Try out a bunch of different options, including things that you would have never considered in the past, until you find one or two (or more) that really stick.

Here are just a few ideas to get you started (but the possibilities are really endless):

- Start running (or walking)

- Play a sport (especially team sports)

- Take a class at the local community college

- Learn a new language

- Take cooking lessons

- Read a good book

- Paint or draw

- Learn a craft

- Go dancing (or learn to dance)

- Start volunteering

- Go to a poetry reading

- Go to an art gallery or museum

- Go hiking

- Go fishing

- Go hunting

- Get a pedicure

- Get a massage

As you can see, there really is no limit on the possibilities. This list is by no means comprehensive. As long as it makes you feel better, doesn't cause you any harm, and doesn't break the bank, do it!

CHAPTER 7: STRATEGY 5 – DOCUMENT EVERYTHING

Bullying in the workplace is not allowed and not tolerated. If the heads of your company learn about bullying, they will (or should) put an end to it. Unfortunately, it can be extremely difficult to prove that bullying is happening. This is especially true if your bully is in a higher position than you.

Because of this, it is important to document everything that happens so that you have a record of what is happening so that when you go to your superiors, you have real documentation to refer to rather than just your memory. This will give your complaints more legitimacy.

Make a regular habit of coming home and writing a sort of journal entry that describes each interaction you had with your bully that day. Note the specific times, and try to be as close to the actual events as possible. Avoid emotional language, except when you are directly stating how a specific event affected you emotionally.

In addition to the journal, consider asking coworkers to write reports of their own about specific situations which they witnessed. Be careful that you ask people you know you can trust. Some might sympathize with the bully or be too scared themselves to help.

Essentially, what you want to create is a clear record with dates, times, locations, and key details of each bullying situation you experience. You also need to include any official documents that you receive or submit, which are related to the bullying. By having a meticulous and well-organized record, you will have a much easier time of proving your case and forcing those who are higher up to actually address the problem.

Keep in mind that you absolutely do not want to keep any part of this record inside the office. Do not write it on your office computer or save it in any office files. Keep all of this documentation at home or somewhere else outside of the office which is safe.

You also don't want to do anything that could be considered an invasion of privacy such as recording interactions with the bully without their knowledge. This is why I stated earlier "only in a public place". Check with the laws in your area, but usually you can record a person without them knowing if you are in a public place, but not in a bathroom, office, or anywhere else that someone else cannot just walk through and start up a conversation.

Instead, just try to make sure that as many of your interactions as possible happen in front of your coworkers. This way, you have witnesses who can verify the abusive treatment. You want to make sure everything you do is above board, legal, and thoroughly detailed so that there is no room for the bully to manipulate, or twist, the story and make you look like the one in the wrong.

This is an important part of your overall approach because this is how you gather the proof that will build a strong case. There are, unfortunately, a lot of companies out there who want to ignore and cover up cases of bullying in their office. This means you need to be able to come to them with a clear and undeniable case that forces them to actually address it. You have the burden of proof here.

If you have the good fortune to be in a company which is more proactive about bullying, and actively tries to cultivate a positive working environment, you'll have an easier time getting your superiors to take your case seriously. You can go to your HR representative and ask them about the company policy toward workplace bullying. Pay attention to the details of the policy, as well as the attitude your HR representative has when you ask about it. This will give you a good idea of about how much support you can expect to get from your company with this issue.

Whether it's going to be easy or difficult, it is still worth pursuing. It's just important to know in advance what your company's attitude toward workplace bullying is so that you have a better idea of how difficult your journey is going to be.

CHAPTER 8: STRATEGY 6 – STAY HEALTHY

As mentioned earlier, your physical health is essential because it is going to give you the strength to endure the challenging situation you are in. Many studies have shown that poor physical health leads to increased stress, mood swings, irritability, and poor control over one's emotions. Poor health also makes you lose focus, have difficulty concentrating, suffer from memory loss, and generally have poorer cognitive functioning.

A poor diet will also send you on peaks and crashes in energy levels that leave you fatigued. All of these factors combined make it difficult to handle a normal work day, let alone the kind of stress you are facing with your bully. This is why it is so important to pay attention to your health.

You don't have to get on a really strict diet and exercise regime, or obsessively count calories, but you do need to eat healthier foods and make time for physical activity.

Here are a few basic guidelines to follow in terms of diet:

✓ Eat 25-30 grams of fiber per day. This means about 9-10 grams of fiber per meal. Fiber helps improve your digestion and detox your system. It also helps regulate blood sugar levels to prevent those spikes and crashes in energy that you feel when you eat a lot of junk. Some good sources of fiber include whole grains, beans, fruits, and vegetables.

✓ Eat 50-60 grams of protein per day. That's about 17-20 grams of protein per meal. Protein is the best source of long term, sustainable energy. A high protein breakfast will prevent midmorning fatigue and cravings. Most people immediately think of meat when they think of protein. Of course, this is a good source of protein but you can also get a lot of healthy protein from beans, oatmeal, yogurt, cheese, and fish.

✓ Eat 10-15 grams of unsaturated fat per day. That's about 3-5 grams of unsaturated fat per meal. Fat has been demonized by many diets, but it is actually very important for your health. You don't need a whole lot of it, but it helps your digestion and is important for brain health. It also helps you process and absorb certain vitamins because some vitamins are "fat soluble", meaning they can only be dissolved and absorbed in fat. Good sources of unsaturated fat include fish, olive oil, coconut oil, and nuts.

By focusing on getting enough of these 3 main nutrients (fiber, protein, and unsaturated fat) from healthy sources, you'll easily start eating a healthier diet, without having to spend all your time counting calories or vitamins. Don't be afraid to experiment with different foods and recipes to find healthy meals that you really enjoy.

You also don't have to give up your guilty pleasures completely. Go ahead and have that slice of cake or that bag of chips. Just don't eat them on a daily basis and definitely do not make them the main source of calories in your diet. You don't want to stress yourself out even more by worrying about your diet and feeling like you failed every time you eat a chocolate bar. Just make sure that your 3 main meals have a healthy balance of the 3 nutrients and try to snack on healthy foods as well. But don't beat yourself up if you like to relax with a scoop of ice cream at night after a stressful day at work.

You will also want to be more active but, again, you don't want to add more stress to your life than you already have by trying to follow a strict workout routine. Instead, just make a little time for physical activity during the week. As a general rule of thumb, you should get at least 20 minutes of exercise per day. This means that you should do some activity that elevates your heart and causes you to break a sweat for at least 20 minutes per day.

Here are a few ideas for being more active:

- Go jogging around your neighborhood in the morning or evening

- Do a combination of pushups, jumping jacks, and lunges each morning or evening.

- Join a sports team

- Go swimming

- Take a kickboxing or self-defense class

- Go biking

- Go hiking in nearby hills

- Take up rock climbing

- Get a treadmill or stationary bike to get exercise while you watch TV.

There are lots of ways that you can stay active without suffering through a bland workout routine. Get creative. Experiment with a few different activities. Mix things up throughout the week or month so that you don't get burnt out on any one activity.

CHAPTER 9: STRATEGY 7 – GET HELP

You should not try to bear the burden of all the stress from your bully alone. Even if you tried, you would not be able to. You are going to need the help of others to actually find a real solution to this problem. You need both emotional support and legal support to make sure you have the strength and means to see this to the end.

Asking for help does not mean you are weak or incapable. It simply means that you acknowledge the power of cooperation and teamwork. Getting help from others will give you the opportunity to have a variety of perspectives on the problem. You'll be exposed to ideas that you might not have had on your own. You'll also be able to feel secure in knowing that you are not alone in this problem.

Bullies usually try to isolate their targets so that they become weaker just as a predator will try to separate their prey from the rest of its pack. By getting help and avoiding isolation, you will be stopping the bully from achieving one of his or her goals.

Therefore, what kind of help do you need? You mainly need it on two fronts. First of all, you will need to seek out sympathetic coworkers and supervisors who can help you navigate the legal, or official, aspects of reporting your bully, and making sure that the company punishes the bullying behavior appropriately. If you find that you have a lack of support in the office, seek outside help from a lawyer or other legal or business consultant who can guide you through the process. One of the things you'll want to ask is what kind of proof and documentation you will need. Find out what sort of information is needed to make a strong case and then immediately start to get and keep track of that information.

Secondly, you want to build a strong emotional support network. That "network" can be one amazing friend who is willing to let you vent as much, and as often, as you want. It can also be a group of trusted friends, families, or even coworkers who care about you. The important thing is that you have at least one person who is understanding and patient and will provide you with emotional support.

When reaching out to coworkers, you'll want to be careful that you don't go to someone who is sympathetic with the bully. It is highly likely that your bully is trying to build up support on his or her side to alienate you in the office. They will do this through lying, manipulation, and coercion, all of which can be very influential. Therefore, take note of how certain people are treating you. Before mentioning your problem, just try to make small talk or discuss business more generally. Pay attention to how they respond. If they seem uncomfortable or distant, this could mean that they have taken the bully's side. Don't blame them or try to start a fight. Just take note that this is not a person you should reach out to.

When reaching out to friends, make sure to ask them if you can vent to them before just launching into it. Be straightforward and let them know that you need someone to talk through your problems with. Good friends will be more than happy to listen to you and talk with you, but it's still a good idea to just make sure they are prepared to be a source of support for you. If possible, reach out to a few different friends, so that you are not putting the full burden on just one person. Whether you have one person or 10, make sure that you talk with them regularly. Anytime you feel that you are starting to get overwhelmed, call one of your trusted friends or relatives to talk through it and level yourself out again.

You can also consider seeing a professional therapist. They can be a huge source of emotional support and help you maintain a clear perspective. A therapist might also become useful in the official process because they can provide an expert opinion on the effects the bullying has had on your life.

Before moving on to the next strategy, there is one final note to make when it comes to asking for help. It seems obvious, but all too often, people tend to take the help they get for granted. So make sure that you show your appreciation to everyone who helps you.

In supporting you, they are willingly taking on a share of the stress that you are experiencing. So make a point to tell them that you value and appreciate what they are doing for you. It is easy to forget such seemingly small things as saying thank you when you are undergoing as much stress, as you are when being bullied. But just try to make a conscious effort to say a heartfelt thank you when you can.

CHAPTER 10: STRATEGY 8 – DON'T BE TOO NICE

While you don't want to respond to your bully with aggression or irritation, you also don't want to be overly complacent either. You need to walk that fine balance between sinking to the bully's level by being mean, and letting yourself get abused and taken advantage of. If you cater too much to your bully, they will only demand more and more out of you. They are trying to beat you into submission, so the last thing you want to do is submit.

Your bully is never going to be satisfied with what you do, even if you meet every single one of the demands they have laid out. So there is no point in attempting to please someone who has made it their goal to never be pleased with you. It will only lead you to taking on more and more work, without getting anymore appreciation or gratitude for the extra effort you are putting in. More importantly, you are not going to defeat your bully through excessive complacence and niceness.

Again, you don't have to be rude. Just be professionally and politely firm in your position. Set clear boundaries and enforce them politely. This is definitely a very challenging strategy to actually execute. Even without a bully, many people have a hard time with setting clear boundaries and making sure that people respect them. With a bully, it can seem like utterly impossible advice to follow.

However, that doesn't mean you should just give up and give in to your bully. Instead, dig your heels in and become even more determined.

Here are a few tips for setting and enforcing your boundaries while remaining polite and respectful:

- ✓ <u>Clearly define your job description</u>: know exactly what it is you are responsible for doing. It is ok (and even encouraged) to take on a little extra responsibility now and then when you are trying to get a promotion. However, you shouldn't allow your bully to put more responsibility on your shoulders than you are obligated to take. If your bully is asking you to do something that falls outside your job description, politely suggest that they talk to the person who is in charge of that aspect of the work.

- ✓ <u>Politely demand specifics</u>: the first time your bully comes to you with a demand, don't let them get away with vague or ambiguous descriptions of what they need. Politely ask questions to clarify the specifics of what they need you to do and then take notes of what they say so that you have notes to reference later when they (almost certainly) try to claim that you didn't do what was asked of you. If they refuse to give you additional information (another scenario that is highly probable), don't lose your temper. Instead, calmly explain how you intend to approach the project and ask them if there is anything they would like to change or add to your planned approach. If they say no, make sure to take note of that. It is even better to do this over email so that you can have a verifiable record of what was said.

✓ Practice the professional "No": if your bully is demanding that you take on work that you shouldn't be responsible for, or insists that you take on more work than you could possibly do in the time frame, you need to muster up the courage to say no. Refuse to take on work that you won't be able to do to the best of your ability. There is a way to say no politely and professionally to avoid accusations of laziness or refusing to do your job. Rather than just saying "no", or "I can't do that", describe the projects and assignments that you are already responsible for, and then politely ask how this new assignment should be prioritized. In other words, ask which other project they would like you to stop doing or delay in order to get this new assignment done in the time frame proposed.

✓ <u>Communicate through email as much as possible</u>: not only does this help you avoid losing your temper and maintain a calm and professional attitude with your bully, it also gives you a written record of your interactions. If a bully demanded one thing of you before, and then tries to claim that they gave you different instructions later on, you can easily refer to the email in which they gave the original instructions. For example, if they tell you to delay one project in favor of another, and then later try to blame you for the delays on the other one, you can refer to the email in which they told you to delay the other project. Furthermore, there will be a written record of the professional and polite way you have been handling the situation.

The emphasis on remaining polite and respectful is important because this is what will separate you from your bully. You want to make sure that you don't lose your temper or your professionalism throughout this process. Your bully is going to be doing everything that he or she can to discredit you and tarnish your reputation. So you need to be extra careful that you maintain a professional and respectful attitude. This way, any lies or rumors that your bully tries to use will fall flat because the others in the office will know that you are not that sort of person.

CHAPTER 11: STRATEGY 9 - BE SMART ABOUT APPROACHING HR & MANAGEMENT

When you have reached the stage where you feel prepared to bring your case to HR and management, you want to make sure that you approach them smartly. This is especially true if you are dealing with a company that has proven to be reluctant to actually address bullying among its employees.

Even if you have a clear and well documented case of bullying to bring before them, you run the risk of getting dismissed if you don't approach them in the correct manner. This is especially true for women who, as mentioned, are quickly written off as overly emotional and sensitive.

If you aren't careful, management might just assume your complaints are just a result of your "feminine nature", rather than real and urgent problems in the workplace. This is even more likely if you work in a company with an overwhelming majority of males in upper management.

If your bully is another female, you will also face the obstacle of proving that she is bullying you. Women are assumed to be nurturing and compassionate so upper management might find it difficult to believe that a woman is even capable of bullying.

It is unfortunate that we are still living in an age where our gender influences the way we are perceived by others, especially in the workplace. However, these are the circumstances we live in and the only way to change them is to fight one battle at a time. Doing what you can to make sure that your case is dealt with properly is one step in the right direction toward creating a business world which is more collaborative, and less divided along gender lines.

So when you approach management and HR with your case, follow these general guidelines:

First, don't make the psychological or emotional harm the focus of your complaint. While it is completely true and extremely important, it is an issue that will likely make them uncomfortable. In a business environment, such nuanced and unquantifiable issues as emotions are usually avoided. So you want to avoid making this the centerpiece of your complaint. That doesn't mean ignore it altogether. Just don't emphasize it as the main point. You don't want the success or failure of your case to depend on whether or not the upper management in your company are sympathetic and compassionate.

Secondly, emphasize quantifiable problems. Focus on how the bullying has affected your work productivity, and thus the productivity of the business. Discuss the concrete ways in which the bully has tried to prevent you from doing your very best at work and how that is affecting the company's bottom line. You can mention the psychological and emotional harm as an aspect of this. In other words, you can mention that this emotional abuse is one of the ways in which the bully is preventing you from fulfilling your maximum potential. By emphasizing these quantifiable problems, you are making it clear that your problems are their problems as well. By decreasing your work productivity, they are losing money. So it would be in their best interest to put a stop to the bullying in order to maximum productivity in their office.

CHAPTER 12: STRATEGY 10 - BRACE YOURSELF FOR A BATTLE

Even if you catch this bullying behavior early on and start to take action immediately, it is not going to be an easy fight. You are going to face a lot of obstacles; as a direct result of the bully and as a result of being a woman in the male-dominated world of business. You might also be in a company that has a bad record of dealing with bullying and does not want to acknowledge any bullying that may be happening in its work environment.

Do not give up at any point. Use every resource you can get your hands on. Do everything in your power to keep fighting. You might not feel like you have the strength to endure a long, drawn out battle right now, but you will find the strength along the way. Use the strategies in this book to help you build up that strength.

You also need to be prepared to walk away. If it becomes clear that management is not willing to deal with this obvious problem, and that they would rather just tolerate bullying, you need to quit. It might be a good idea to start looking for other opportunities as soon as you begin developing your action plan for dealing with the bully. Even knowing that you have a backup plan can be a great source of motivation and confidence when dealing with the problem at your current job.

Don't openly look for other jobs. Just do this on the side. If it does reach the point where you have to quit, make it very clear exactly why you are quitting. You shouldn't remain silent or let them cover up the bullying issue. Make sure there is no ambiguity. You are taking another job because this office tolerates bullying. Hopefully, this can help inspire them to change their attitude toward workplace bullying in the future.

Whatever happens, you can do this. You will get through this and you will find a way to make your work life less stressful, and less emotionally taxing. You deserve a work environment that encourages you to do your best, not one that holds you down and disrespects you.

Unfortunately, it's not going to be easy to get that when you are dealing with a bully. It is a difficult battle, but it is one that is 100% worth fighting. You will be a stronger and happier person for having gone through this difficult and trying experience.

CHAPTER 13: CONCLUSION

After learning more about workplace bullying in this book, you hopefully have learned two things. First, this is by no means a simple or easy issue. You will face many obstacles and roadblocks. You will be told to "suck it up", or told that your complaints are unreasonable. It's going to be tough.

Secondly, even though it's tough, it *is* possible. By using the strategies that you have read about in the previous chapters, you will be able to deal with workplace bullying effectively. You will find a way to eliminate that stress and anxiety from your life and create or find a work environment that is cooperative and encouraging rather than violently competitive and negative.

The 10 strategies you have read about in this book were specifically chosen to make sure that you balance practical external action with strength-building internal solutions. The strategies that focus on your emotional, psychological, and physical health are all meant to accomplish a few things:

- ✓ Minimize the long term damage that can be caused by bullying
- ✓ Build up the individual strength that is needed in order to deal with this issue
- ✓ Minimize the risk of acting against your own best interest

The strategies that focus on finding meaningful ways of getting rid of the bully, or making sure that he or she is punished, accomplish other important goals like:

- ✓ Putting a stop to your own bullying

✓ Discouraging other potential bullies from targeting you, or anyone else in the office

✓ Helping to create a positive, bully-free workplace environment

Therefore, get ready to tackle this problem from every angle and resolve it once and for all! It will be a tough fight but you will be able to build up the strength and tenacity that you need along the way and you will walk away from this stronger and happier than you were.

ABOUT THE AUTHOR

Natalie Disque is a PMP certified full time IT Project Manager who has worked in the IT department for many clients such as Capital One, Bank of America, Wells Fargo, Prudential Relocation, and Johnson & Johnson Canada. Due to her many business contracts throughout the years, Natalie has learned the fine art of negotiating. This book includes just some of the main 25 negotiating strategies as a woman that she believes you should know and use to get what you want in life.

Natalie resides in the Chesterfield Virginia area. You can connect with Natalie on LinkedIn: https://www.linkedin.com/pub/natalie-disque-pmp/5/202/717